California
Facts and Symbols

by Emily McAuliffe

Content Consultant:
Gary F. Kurutz
Curator of Special Collections
California State Library

Hilltop Books

An Imprint of Franklin Watts
A Division of Grolier Publishing
New York London Hong Kong Sydney
Danbury, Connecticut

Hilltop Books
http://publishing.grolier.com

Library of Congress Cataloging-in-Publication Data
McAuliffe, Emily.
    California facts and symbols/by Emily McAuliffe.
    p.cm.--(The states and their symbols)
    Includes bibliographical references and index.
    Summary: Presents information about the state of California, its nickname,
motto, and emblems.
    ISBN 1-56065-763-4
    1. Emblems, State--California--Juvenile literature. [1. Emblems,
State--California. 2. California.] I. Title. II. Series: McAuliffe, Emily.
States and their symbols.
CR203.C2M38 1998
979.4--DC21
                                                              97-40419
                                                                 CIP
                                                                  AC

Editorial credits:
Editor, Cara Van Voorst; additional editing, Kim Covert; cover design, Clay
    Schotzko/Icon Productions; illustrations, James Franklin; photo research,
    Michelle L. Norstad.

Photo credits:
Images International/Erwin C. "Bud" Nielsen, 18
One Mile Up, Inc., 8, 10 (inset)
Chuck Place, 14, 16
Unicorn Stock Photos/Joseph Sohm, cover; Dick Young, 6; Andre Jenny, 10; Dede
    Gilman, 12, 20; Jean Higgins, 22 (top); Gerald Lim, 22 (middle); H. Schmeiser,
    22 (bottom)

Table of Contents

Fast Facts about California

Capital: Sacramento is the capital of California.

Largest City: Los Angeles is the largest city in California. About three and one-half million people live in Los Angeles.

Size: California covers 163,707 square miles (425,638 square kilometers).

Location: California is on the western coast of the United States. It is bordered by Oregon, Nevada, Arizona, and Mexico.

Population: 31,878,234 people live in California (U.S. Census Bureau, 1996 estimate).

Statehood: California became the 31st state on September 9, 1850.

Natural Resources: California's natural resources include oil, fish, gold, and natural gas.

Manufactured Goods: Californians make aircraft, films, computers, newspapers, and food products.

Crops: California farmers grow cotton, rice, grapes, and fruits and vegetables.

State Name and Nickname

A Spanish man wrote a book about an imaginary island. He wrote the book about 500 years ago. The island in his book was full of gold. He named it California.

Spanish explorers came to the area that is now California. An explorer travels an area to discover what it is like. Spanish explorers thought the land looked like the island in the book. They named the land California.

California's nickname is the Golden State. People call California the Golden State for two reasons. Miners found gold in California during the mid-1800s. Miners still find gold in California. Many golden poppies also grow in California. These flowers give the land a golden look.

Miners still find gold in California.

State Seal and Motto

The state seal is a small picture pressed into wax. Government officials stamp the state seal on important papers. The seal makes government papers official.

The state seal is a symbol. A symbol is an object that reminds people of something larger. For example, the U.S. flag reminds people of the United States.

California adopted its seal in 1849. The woman on the seal is Minerva. She is the Roman goddess of wisdom. The grizzly bear stands for wildlife. The grapes stand for good farmland. The gold miner is an important part of California's history.

Thirty-one stars appear on the seal. Each star on the seal stands for one state. California became a state in 1850. It was the 31st state to join the United States.

California's state motto is Eureka. A motto is a word or saying. Eureka means I have found it. Miners said eureka when they found gold in California.

California adopted its seal in 1849.

State Capitol and Flag

Sacramento is the capital of California. A capital is the city where government is based.

The capitol building is also in Sacramento. Government officials work at the capitol. Some officials make laws for the state. Others make sure the laws are carried out.

Workers completed the capitol in 1869. It is four stories high. Workers added a new part in 1952. The new part is six stories high. Officials work in the old and new parts of the building.

California's flag flies above the capitol. John Fremont helped create the flag in 1846. He and other American settlers carried the flag into battle against Mexico in 1846. The flag showed a big, brown grizzly bear. The California government adopted this flag in 1911. Today, people call it the California Bear flag.

The bear on the flag stands for strength. A red star and stripe appear on the flag. They stand for bravery.

California's capitol is in Sacramento.

State Bird

The California valley quail became the state bird in 1931. The California valley quail has brown, gray, and green feathers. It has a white belly. The quail has a white stripe on its head and neck. The stripe looks like a small crown. Six black feathers stick out of the quail's head.

Quails travel in large groups during fall and winter. Quails squawk loudly when enemies come near. Then the birds fly off in many directions. Foxes, owls, hawks, and raccoons hunt quails. People also hunt the birds.

Quails travel in pairs during spring. Males and females find places to make their nests. California valley quails make their nests in the ground. They dig holes and line them with leaves and grass. Adult quails eat seeds, grass, fruit, and flies.

Female quails lay six to 28 eggs. The eggs are creamy white with golden-brown spots.

The California valley quail has a white stripe on its head and neck.

State Tree

The California redwood tree became the state tree in 1937. Two kinds of redwood trees are state trees. One is the coast redwood. The other is the giant sequoia.

Coast redwoods are the tallest living things on Earth. The tallest coast redwood is 385 feet (117 meters) high. Giant sequoias are also huge. Their trunks are up to 30 feet (9 meters) across.

The General Sherman Tree is the world's largest giant sequoia. It stands in Sequoia National Park. The tree is 275 feet (84 meters) high. It is 36.5 feet (11 meters) across. This tree may be more than 3,000 years old.

The U.S. government protects some California redwoods. Protect means to keep safe. Protected redwood trees grow in special areas. People cannot cut down redwood trees in these areas.

Coast redwoods are the tallest living things on Earth.

State Flower

California's state flower is the golden poppy. State government officials chose the golden poppy on April 6, 1903.

Golden poppies grow wild throughout California. People also grow golden poppies in their gardens.

Golden poppies bloom from June to October. Bloom means to flower. Cup of gold is one nickname for golden poppies.

Poppy seeds are food for people and animals. Bakers sprinkle poppy seeds on bread and rolls. Companies make cooking oil from the seeds. Companies also use poppy seeds to make food for birds and cattle.

Californians now observe California Poppy Day on April 6 every year. Some areas hold special fairs on Poppy Day.

Golden poppies grow wild throughout California.

State Animal

The California grizzly bear became California's state animal in 1953. But grizzly bears do not live in California anymore. A farmer killed California's last known grizzly in 1922.

California grizzly bears are huge brown bears. They weigh up to 400 pounds (180 kilograms). Some grizzlies are 12 feet (3.7 meters) tall.

Grizzly bears eat plants, nuts, wild fruits, fish, and berries. They also eat insects. An insect is a small animal with six legs. Grizzlies work hard to find insects to eat. They tear apart old logs to find them.

Most California grizzly bears sleep through the winter. They build their dens in the fall. Some grizzlies dig dens under the roots of big trees. Others dig dens in the ground or use caves as dens. The bears stay in their dens from October to March. They live on the fat stored in their bodies.

Grizzly bears do not live in California anymore.

More State Symbols

State Fish: The South Fork golden trout is California's state fish. The golden trout lives in lakes and streams.

State Fossil: The saber-toothed cat is California's state fossil. The saber-toothed cat was larger than a modern lion.

State Gemstone: Benitoite is California's state gemstone. People call benitoite the blue diamond. The only known supply of benitoite is in San Benito County.

State Mineral: Gold is California's state mineral. Gold is very valuable. People have paid up to $850 for one ounce (28 grams) of gold.

State Reptile: The desert tortoise is California's state reptile. The desert tortoise lives in California's southwestern desert areas.

State Marine Mammal: The California Gray Whale is California's state marine mammal. The California legislature chose the California Gray Whale in 1975. These whales travel along California's coast.

The desert tortoise is California's state reptile.

Places to Visit

Redwood National Park

Redwood National Park is near Crescent City. The park opened in 1965. The tallest tree in the world stands in the park. This coast redwood is 385 feet (117 meters) high. It is more than 600 years old. Visitors fish, camp, picnic, swim, and hike in the park. They also see the giant redwoods.

Sea World

Sea World is a park in San Diego. Visitors see many shows and displays about ocean life. A popular show features killer whales. Trainers teach killer whales to do tricks. Trainers ride on the backs of the whales. The whales jump up and splash onlookers.

Alcatraz Island

Alcatraz Island is in San Francisco Bay. Workers built a prison on the island in 1859. Prisoners lived in Alcatraz until it closed in 1963. People called the prison The Rock. Workers built the prison on a large rocky area. Visitors tour the prison and learn about the island's history.

Words to Know

bloom (BLOOM)—to flower

explorer (ek-SPLOR-ur)—a person who travels an area to discover what it is like

fossil (FOSS-uhl)—the remains of an animal or plant that lived long ago

gem (JEM)—a rare and valued stone

insect (IN-sekt)—a small animal with six legs

mammal (MAM-uhl)—a warm-blooded animal with a backbone

motto (MOT-oh)—a word or saying

protect (pruh-TECT)—to keep safe

symbol (SIM-buhl)—an object that reminds people of something larger

Read More

Bock, Judy and Rachel Kranz. *Scholastic Encyclopedia of the United States*. New York: Scholastic, 1997.

Capstone Press Geography Department. *California*. One Nation. Mankato, Minn.: Capstone Press, 1998.

Fradin, Dennis B. *California*. From Sea to Shining Sea. Chicago: Children's Press, 1993.

Krensky, Stephen. *Striking it Rich: The Story of the California Gold Rush*. New York: Simon & Schuster, 1996.

Useful Addresses

California Secretary of State
1500 11th Street
Sacramento, California 95814

California Division of Tourism
P.O. Box 1499
Department TIA
Sacramento, CA 95812

Internet Sites

A Brief Guide to State Facts
http://phoenix.ans.se/freeweb/holly/state.html#california
California Insignia
http://library.ca.gov/california/cahinsig.html
50 States and Capitals
http://www.scvol.com/States/main.htm

Index